3 3197 00484642 9

921
HOW

Howe, James.

Playing with words

604697 01395   13375D

PLAYING
WITH WORDS

by

James Howe

photographs by

Michael Craine

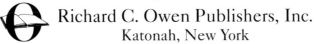

Richard C. Owen Publishers, Inc.
Katonah, New York

Meet the Author titles

Verna Aardema *A Bookworm Who Hatched*
Jean Fritz *Surprising Myself*
Paul Goble *Hau Kola Hello Friend*
Lee Bennett Hopkins *The Writing Bug*
James Howe *Playing with Words*
Rafe Martin *A Storyteller's Story*
Patricia Polacco *Firetalking*
Cynthia Rylant *Best Wishes*
Jane Yolen *A Letter from Phoenix Farm*

Text copyright © 1994 by James Howe
Photographs copyright © 1994 by Michael Craine

Richard C. Owen Publishers, Inc.
P.O. Box 585
Katonah, New York 10536

Library of Congress Cataloging-in-Publication Data

Howe , James .
      Playing with words / by James Howe ; photographs by Michael
Craine .
         p .   cm . — (Meet the author)
      ISBN 1-878450-40-9 : $12.95
         1 . Howe , James — Biography — Juvenile literature .
2 . Authors , American — 20th century — Biography — Juvenile literature .
3 . Children's stories — Authorship — Juvenile literature . [1 . Howe ,
James . 1946 . 2 . Authors , American] I . Craine , Michael , ill .
II . Title . III . Series : Meet the author (Katonah , N . Y .)
PS3558 . 08923Z466   1994
813 ' . 54 — dc20
[B]   93-48166

The text type was set in Caslon 540.
Editor-in-Chief/Art Director Janice Boland

Printed in the United States of America

9 8 7 6 5 4 3 2

To my readers

When I was young, I loved playing with words.
So did everyone in my family.
I learned early that if I was going
to keep up with my three older brothers,
I had to make them laugh.
Words were the best way I knew to do that.
Still, I never dreamed that
I could turn my words into books
and one day make a living from them.
I was thirty when I wrote my first book, *Bunnicula*,
and I wrote it just for fun.

Center CHAPTER 3 — Some Unusual ~~Goings-On~~ whose curiosity had been aroused by the strange behavior of the rabbit that first night 17

The next few days passed uneventfully. I was very bored. Chester had decided to stay awake every night, to observe him. Therefore he too spent most of his days sleeping, as he was up every night watching the rabbit: and had no one to talk to.

Finally, on the morning of the fourth day, I caught Chester bleary-eyed over the water dish. "Anything new to report, Sherlock?" I would ask him each morning.

~~Chester, who was always bleary-eyed when I was just getting up from a~~

He good night's sleep, ~~would~~ grumble at me in a most unpleasant manner.

"You know, Chester, you never were exactly charming in the morning, but lately you've become downright grumpy."

Chester growled in response.

"What are you doing this for anyway? What are you looking for? He's just a cute little bunny!"

was amazed at my character analysis,

"Cute little bunny!" Chester said. "That's what you think. He's a danger to this household and everyone in it."

"Oh, Chester," I said, with an indulgent smile, "I think perhaps it's time you reading has gone to your head," ~~stopped reading Edgar Allen Poe."~~

Bunnicula, a vampire rabbit who attacks vegetables,
was a character I created because
I loved watching vampire movies on TV.
When I was ten, I founded a club
with my two best friends, called the Vampire Legion.
It wasn't until I'd written
two more books after *Bunnicula*
that I started thinking of myself as a writer.
Now I write every day. It's my job,
and I still have fun doing it.

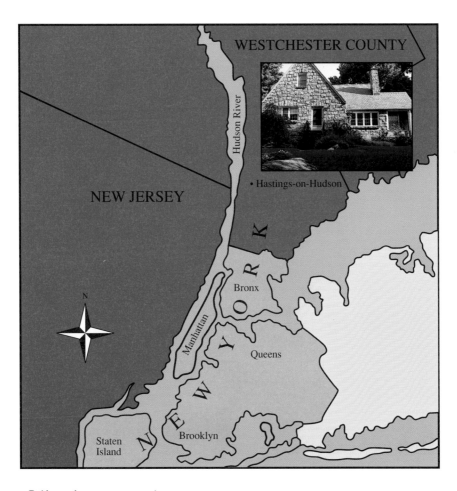

I live in a stone house
in the small town of Hastings-on-Hudson,
a few miles north of New York City.
Many of the people who live here work in the arts.
There are children's book authors and illustrators,
musicians, painters, photographers,
filmmakers, actors, dancers, book editors,
and television producers.

My wife Betsy Imershein is a photographer
and has created several children's books of her own.
We have offices next to each other
on the first floor of our house.

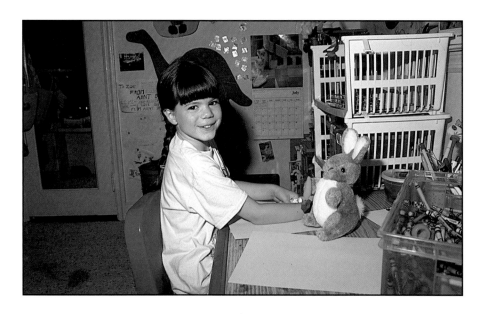

Our daughter Zoe has a playroom down the hall.
She thinks of her playroom as her office,
and she's a frequent visitor to ours.

We both love taking a break to read together.
When the weather's warm, we go outside and read
on our "reading rock" in front of our house.

Every work day usually starts out the same for me.
After feeding our cat Freckle,
getting Zoe off to school, and exercising,
I have breakfast.
Then I take my thermos of coffee and my favorite mug
and walk to the other end
of the house to begin work.

I don't start writing right away.

First I need to open my mind to my work.

I read for a while. Sometimes I draw.

Sometimes I just sit quietly
and jot down ideas and thoughts.
Or I go back and forth doing all these things.

When I'm ready to write,
I reread what I wrote the day before.
Then I edit or rewrite it.
This gets me thinking about
what to do next with my story,
and I don't have to face a blank page
or an empty computer screen first thing.
I enjoy listening to music while I work.
Classical music is best when I'm concentrating,
but country music is my favorite.

Some mornings, I take care of business details.
I make phone calls, answer my mail,
and look over artwork.

I usually eat lunch at home, chatting with Betsy
or reading the newspaper if I'm by myself.
Some days I have lunch with writer friends
at the Center Restaurant,
the most popular meeting place in town.
I never know who might drop by to say hello.

After lunch, I do errands or drop by the public library
or local bookstore to do research or to browse.

I love bookstores and could spend hours in them.
It's almost impossible for me to walk out of one
without having bought at least one book!

If I haven't been away from my office for too long,
I take a short walk
before settling into my afternoon routine.
I carry a pocket notebook and pen with me
because ideas come while I'm walking.
Walks give me a chance to daydream.
Daydreaming is one of the most important things
a writer does;
so is reading.

I spend at least an hour a day reading.
Reading gets me thinking about my own writing
and makes me eager to get back to work.

Some days I take the train to New York City.
I meet with editors and art directors
to discuss ideas for books,
or go over the design and layout of a book,
or look at the work an illustrator has just sent in.

Sometimes I go to the New York Public Library
to do research or visit museums to look at the art.

One of my favorite things
to do in New York City
is find a place among
people where I can write
and draw for long
stretches of time.
Museums are good places
for this.
So are cafés and coffee
shops.

Because Betsy also works at home,
we often talk with each other about our work.
She is the first editor on all my books.
I never show her my work until
I've finished the first draft.
Then I go somewhere else while she reads it.
Knowing that she's reading something
I've just written makes me nervous.
Betsy puts paper clips on the pages
she wants to discuss with me.
If she hands the manuscript back to me
and it feels much heavier
than when I gave it to her,
I know I'm in trouble.
We sit down and go over the manuscript,
page by page, paper clip by paper clip.

My family and my writing are the most important
things in my life.
Since Zoe was born, I've done much less travelling.
I still go to bookstores to sign books
because I love to talk with my readers.
Once or twice a year I take part in conferences
for librarians, teachers, or writers.
When I write speeches for these conferences,
I think about what I want to do next as a writer.

"What's next?" There are endless possibilities.
My *Bunnicula* books are very popular
and I enjoy writing as Harold,
my shaggy-dog narrator.
But over the years
I've created many other characters
and done many other kinds of writing.

My Pinky and Rex series is about two best friends,
a boy and a girl, who are seven.
Many of these stories are based on my own childhood.
Even though I don't share his favorite color,
Pinky is a lot like me: smart in school,
not great in sports, and trying to be himself
even when it means being different from others.

Some of the things that happen to him in the stories
really happened to me,
such as the time he has an embarrassing accident
in front of the whole class
when he wins a spelling bee.
His best friend Rex is based on a girl named Bobbie,
who was my own best friend when I was seven.

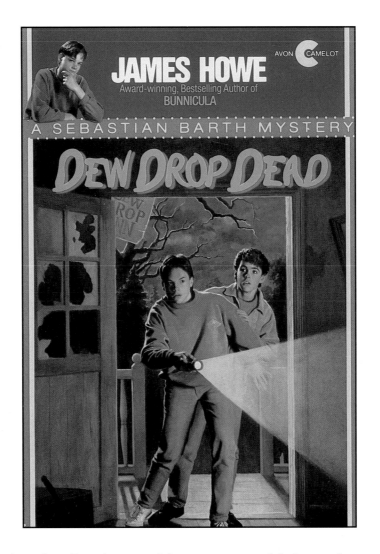

Sebastian Barth, my thirteen-year-old detective,
is the kind of kid I would have *liked* to have been:
cool, clever, and sure of himself.
I've created mysteries for him that are fun
to write and even more fun to solve.

I've written serious books like
I Wish I Were a Butterfly,
and funny books like
The Day the Teacher Went Bananas.
I've written nonfiction, too.
When I was young, I wanted to be an actor.
I studied acting in college
and directing in graduate school.
Once in a while I do some writing that's related
to the theater, movies, and television.
I've written television scripts
for the Disney Channel
and books for children based on movie stories.
My favorite is *Dances With Wolves*.

I don't know what I'll write next.
But whatever it is, I hope I'll be surprised.
Surprise is what keeps readers turning the pages
and writers filling them up.
I'm still surprised sometimes to think
that I became a writer.
When I read letters from my readers that say,
"I'm thinking of becoming a writer, too,"
I wonder, "Will I read your books one day?"
I know it's possible because it happened to me . . .
and all because I loved playing with words.

Other books by James Howe

Bunnicula; Howliday Inn; Nighty-Nightmare; The Celery Stalks at Midnight; There's a Monster Under My Bed; Eat Your Poison, Dear; Hot Fudge; Morgan's Zoo; Pinky and Rex Get Married; Scared Silly.

About the Photographer

Michael Craine is a freelance photographer. He lives in Westchester County, New York. Michael studied photography at The Germane School of Photography and The New School in New York City.

Acknowledgments

Photographs on pages 4 and 26 appear courtesy of James Howe. Illustration on page 5 of Bunnicula vignette from back cover of *Harold and Chester in Hot Fudge* by James Howe, illustrated by Leslie Morrill, illustrations © 1990 by Leslie Morrill, permission granted by Morrow Junior Books, a division of William Morrow and Company, Inc. Manuscript from *Bunnicula* on page 6 appears courtesy of James Howe. Illustrations on page 12 appear courtesy of James Howe. Illustration on page 25 by Werner Blaebst appears courtesy of James Howe. Illustration on page 27 of *Pinky & Rex and the Spelling Bee* by James Howe, illustrated by Melissa Sweet, illustration ©1991 Melissa Sweet, reprinted with permission of Atheneum Publishers, an imprint of Macmillan Publishing. Book cover on page 28 from *Dew Drop Dead* copyright ©1990 is the Avon Book edition cover, which was reprinted by arrangement with Atheneum Publishers.